This book belongs to:

OXFORD

UNIVERSITY PRESS

Great Clarendon Street, Oxford OX2 6DP

Oxford University Press is a department of the University of Oxford.
It furthers the University's objective of excellence in research, scholarship, and education by publishing worldwide.
Oxford is a registered trade mark of Oxford University Press in the UK and in certain other countries

First published 2014
First published in paperback 2015

British Library Cataloguing in Publication Data
Data available

ISBN: 978-0-19-273690-1 (hardback with CD)
ISBN: 978-0-19-273991-9 (hardback)
ISBN: 978-0-19-273691-8 (paperback with CD)
ISBN: 978-0-19-273896-7 (eBook)

1 2 3 4 5 6 7 8 9 10

for Everyone

Printed in China

Paper used in the production of this book is a natural, recyclable product
made from wood grown in sustainable forests.
The manufacturing process conforms to the environmental regulations
of the country of origin.

The drawings in this book were created using pencil, calligraphy
ink, wax crayon, and chalk pastel. They were collaged and coloured
using QuarkXPress and Photoshop.

Thank you to everyone at OUP for their enthusiasm and support
for this project, especially Peter Marley and Harriet Rogers.

tim hopgood

WHAT A
WONDERFUL
WORLD

Based on the song by Bob Thiele &
George David Weiss

OXFORD

UNIVERSITY PRESS

I see trees of green.

Red roses too.

I see them bloom
for me and you.

And I think to myself . . .

What a **WONDERFUL** world.

I see skies of blue . . .

and clouds of white.

The bright blessed day . . .

the dark
sacred
night.

And I think to myself . . .

What a WONDERFUL world.

The colours of the rainbow, so pretty in the sky . . .

are also on the faces
of people going by.

I see friends
shaking hands,
saying,

'How do
you do?'

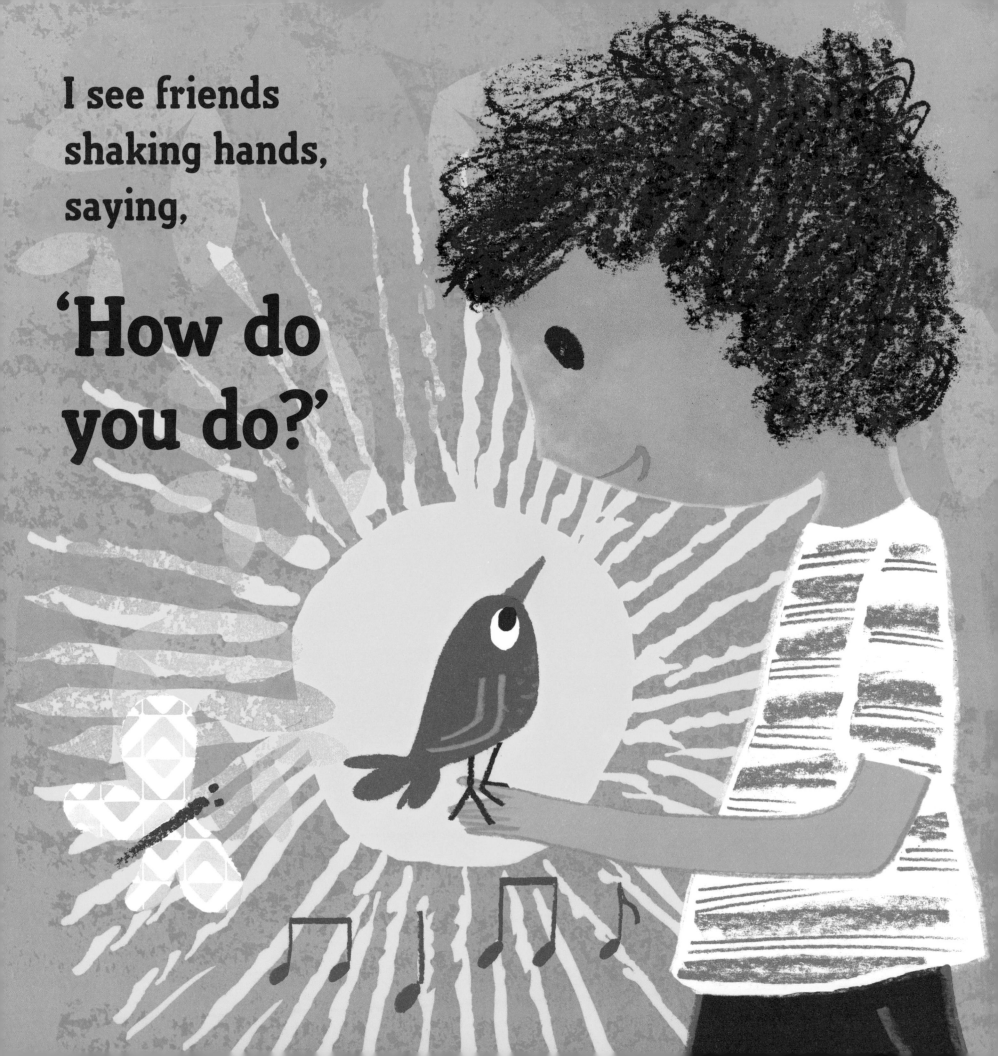

They're really saying, 'I love ♥

you!'

I hear babies cry.
I watch them grow.

They'll learn much more
than I'll ever know.

And I think to myself . . .

What a
WONDERFUL
world.

Yes, I think to myself . . .

What a Wonderful World
was recorded in 1967
by Louis Armstrong
Directed by Tommy Goodman
Produced by Bob Thiele

The recording was inducted into the
Grammy Hall of Fame in 1999

What a Wonderful World
by Bob Thiele and George David Weiss

I see trees of green, red roses too.
I see them bloom for me and you.
And I think to myself,
What a wonderful world.

I see skies of blue and clouds of white.
The bright blessed day; the dark sacred night.
And I think to myself,
What a wonderful world.

The colours of the rainbow, so pretty in the sky,
Are also on the faces of people going by.
I see friends shaking hands, saying,
'How do you do?'
They're really saying, 'I love you'.

I hear babies cry. I watch them grow.
They'll learn much more than I'll ever know.
And I think to myself,
What a wonderful world.

Yes, I think to myself,
What a wonderful world.

I was six years old when I first heard Louis Armstrong's recording of **What a Wonderful World**. We learnt to sing the song at school, and the lyrics made a huge impression on me. It's a song full-to-the-brim with hope and optimism and I think that's what gives it such a timeless quality. A few years ago my daughter found a recording of the song in a flea market, and gave it to me as a present. As soon as I heard Louis Armstrong's gravelly voice sing the first few lines I knew I wanted to capture the joy of the song in a picture book.

timhopgood